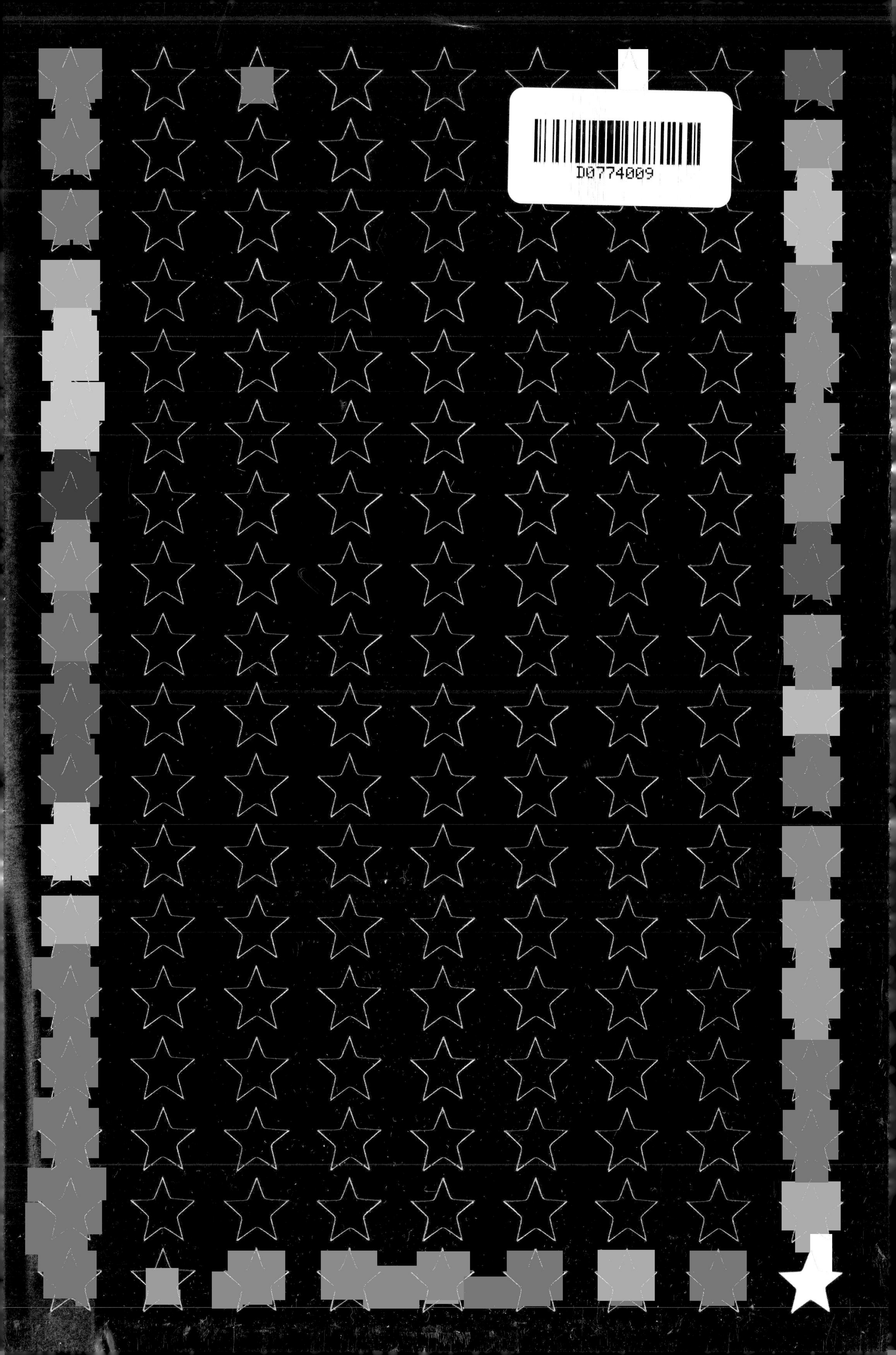
D0774009

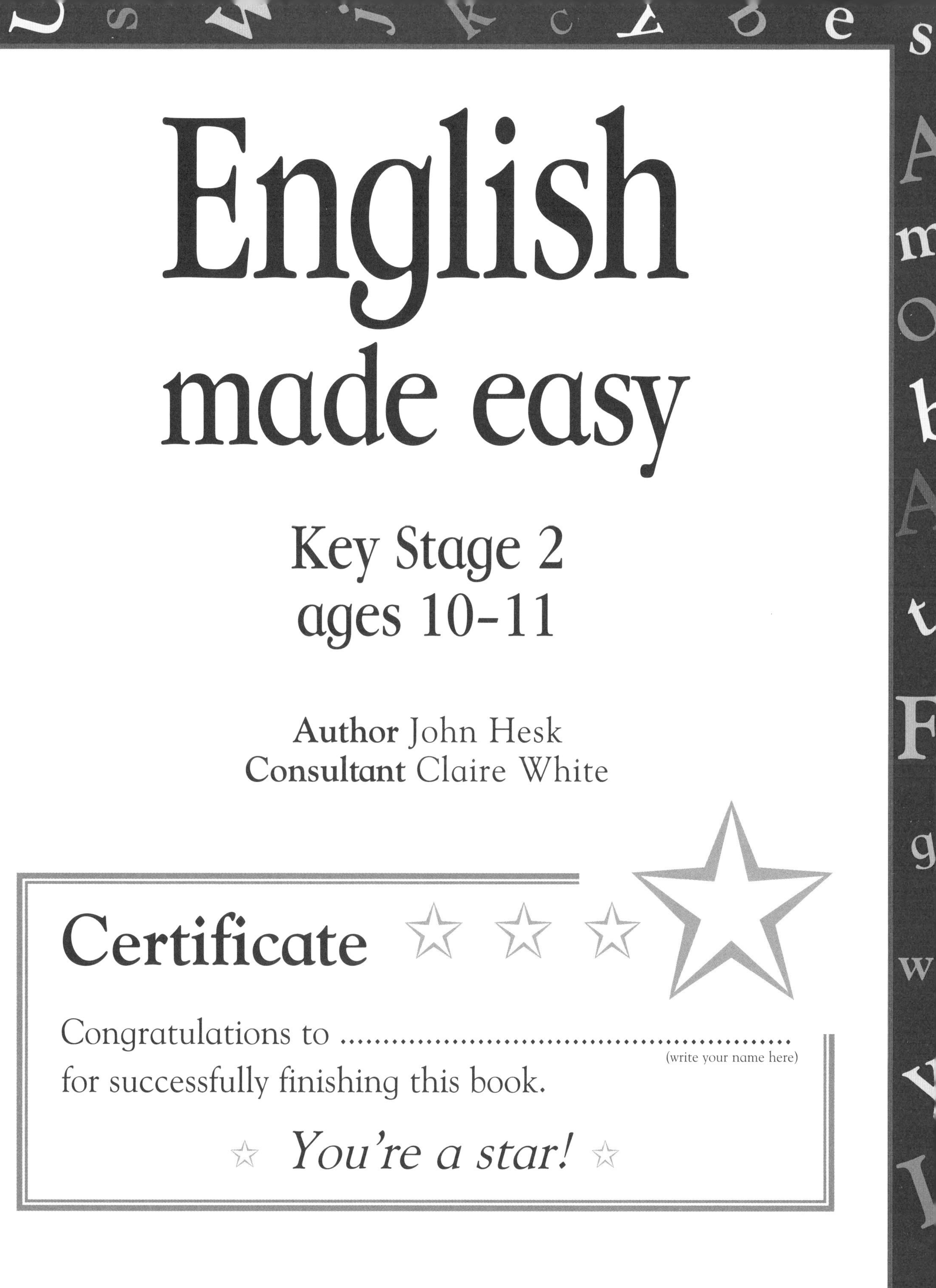

English made easy

Key Stage 2
ages 10–11

Author John Hesk
Consultant Claire White

Certificate

Congratulations to ....
(write your name here)
for successfully finishing this book.

☆ *You're a star!* ☆

LONDON • NEW YORK • MUNICH • MELBOURNE • DELHI

Riddles

Can you solve this word-building **riddle**?

My first is in **bread** but not in **bead**.
My second is in **dig** but not in **dug**.
My third is in **fled** but not in **flew**.
My fourth is in **hid** but not in **hit**.
My fifth is in **held** but not in **herd**.
My sixth is in **step** but not in **stop**.

Answer ....

Now try this one.

My first is in **bite** but not in **site**.
My second is in **tent** but not in **tint**.
My third is in **grow** but not in **brow**.
My fourth is in **in** but not in **on**.
My fifth is in **ton** but not in **tow**.
My sixth is in **stone** but not in **store**.
My seventh is in **pin** but not in **pun**.
My eighth is in **naught** but not in **caught**.
My ninth is in **grip** but not in **drip**.

Answer ....

Try to make some word-building **riddles** of your own. Choose from the list of words below. The first one has been started for you. Continue your **riddles** on an extra sheet of paper.

business	colonel	family	friend	height	necessary
immediate	medicine	neighbour	occasion	queue	rhythm
separate	skilful	twelfth	weird	yacht	

My first is in **bite** but not in **mite**.
My second is in **cup** but not in **cap**.
My third is in **sew** but not in **dew**.
My fourth is in **in** but not in **an**.
My fifth is in **ton** but not in **toe**.

My sixth is in .... but not in ....

My seventh is in .... but not in ....

My eighth is in .... but not in ....

Opposites

Read this **poem** aloud.

Some Opposites

What is the opposite of *riot*?
It's *lots of people keeping quiet.*

The opposite of *doughnut*? Wait
A minute while I meditate.
This isn't easy. Ah, I've found it!
A cookie with a hole around it.

What is the opposite of *two*?
A lonely me, a lonely you.

The opposite of a cloud could be
A white reflection in the sea,
Or a huge blueness in the air,
Caused by a cloud's not being there.

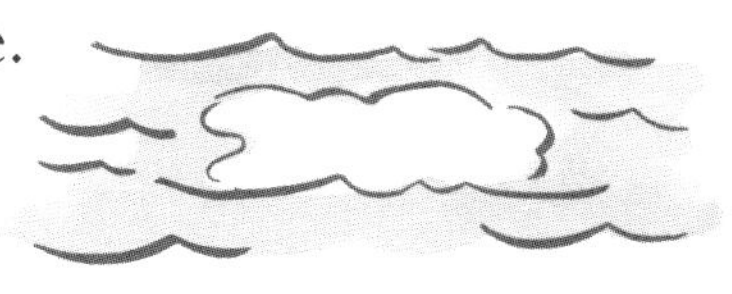

The opposite of *opposite*?
That's much too difficult. I quit.

Richard Wilbur

In the list below, underline the words that can have **opposites**, and draw a ring around those that cannot. Then write down the underlined words and their **opposites**.

far door blue wrong grass quickly pencil light
happy fridge ten town small computer duck

far - near,

Now look at the words you have ringed. Pick three, and make up **words** or **phrases** that could be "joke" **opposites** for them. Write your "joke" **opposites** and your reasons below.

door - wall (a wall is what is left if you have no door!)

You may have found words that cannot even have "joke" **opposites**. Write them here.

Spoonerisms

Kinquering congs is a well-known example of a **spoonerism**. W. A. Spooner from Oxford, England, accidentally "invented" **spoonerisms**: he often mixed up the sounds at the beginning of his words.

What did W. A. Spooner mean to say instead of kinquering congs?

....

Here are some modern **spoonerisms** for you to "translate" into English – take care with the spelling! D

Did you hear the roar-bell ding?

....

Don't forget to dock the law!

....

We had thick frog last fiday.

....

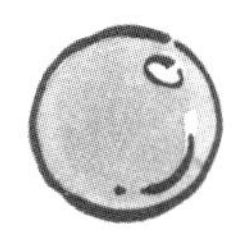

Do you like to bead in red?

....

I can fee my sootprints!

....

I caught a ban of lemon drink.

....

Can you think of any **spoonerisms** yourself? Write them here.

....

....

....

....

Malapropisms

Mrs. Malaprop is a character in a play by R. B. Sheridan. She often gets her words mixed up, using a word that sounds almost, but not quite, like the correct one. For instance, she says the word **allegory** when she means to say **alligator!**

Look up the word **allegory** in the dictionary, then explain the obvious difference between **allegory** and **alligator**. D

....

....

....

Here are some **malapropisms** for you to correct – draw a ring around the word that is used incorrectly, then rewrite the sentence using the correct word. D

There are three angels in a triangle.

....

We decided to sign the partition.

....

I am pleased to except this prize.

....

The brakes on a bike work by fraction.

....

The jugular prepared to pounce.

....

Now find the meanings of the words you ringed, and write them here. D

....

....

....

....

....

....

More malapropisms

The character Dogberry is a Watchman (like a policeman) in Shakespeare's play *Much Ado About Nothing*. He is a memorable comic character because he uses malapropisms in his speech.

Here are some lines from Act III Scene 5.
Underline in Dogberry's lines below the six malapropisms he uses.

LEONATO: What would you with me, honest neighbour?

DOGBERRY: Marry, sir, I would have some confidence with you that decerns you nearly.

LEONATO: Brief, I pray you, for you see it is a busy time with me.

DOGBERRY: Yea, an't 'twere a thousand pound more than 'tis, for I hear as good exclamation on your worship as of any man in the city; and though I be but a poor man, I am glad to hear it.

LEONATO: I would fain know what you have to say.

DOGBERRY: One word, sir: our watch, sir, have indeed comprehended two aspicious persons, and we would have them this morning examined before your worship.

LEONATO: Take their examination yourself and bring it me; I am now in great haste, as it may appear unto you.

DOGBERRY: It shall be suffigance.

Write the meanings of these words that Dogberry meant to use. D

conference ....

concern ....

acclamation ....

apprehended ....

suspicious ....

sufficient ....

Words that confuse

In the piece of writing below, many words sound right but are spelt incorrectly – the wrong homophone has been used. Read through the passage, underlining each wrong word. Then rewrite the passage with the correct spellings. D

Could I survive on a desert aisle? I wood make a hut on the beech from steaks and bits of would. Their would knot bee thyme to get board. I mite try in vein two escape, waiving at plains or passing ships. My hare would grow long. I might have to sow up a peace of sale from my wrecked boat to make knew clothes – a reel site four saw eyes!

....

....

....

....

....

....

The following words are often confused. Write a sentence to show the meaning for each word. D

affect ....

effect ....

eligible ....

illegible ....

cereal ....

serial ....

compliment ....

complement ....

Inventing words

Use a **dictionary** to complete these **definitions**. D

A micro chip is a very small chip of silicone.

A microprocessor is a ....

....

A .... is the climate of a very small area.

A .... is a very small living thing.

An instrument used to look at very small objects is a ....

Find three more words beginning with the **prefix** micro- and explain their meanings. D

A micro .... is ....

A micro .... is ....

A micro .... is ....

Now make up some new "micro" words, and **define** them. For example, a microsnack is a snack that is too small to be satisfying but too tasty to resist.

....

....

Complete these **definitions**.

A mega byte is a very large unit of computer memory.

A megaphone is a ....

A megamouth is a shark with a ....

A megalopolis is a ....

A .... is a very large stone or rock.

Now make up some "mega" words, and **define** them. For example, a megamouse is an extra-large mouse from the planet Megary.

....

....

Information text

Although pirates in stories are often portrayed as lovable rogues, the real-life pirates who sailed the oceans searching out laden ships were usually ruthless robbers. Read the following historical information about real pirates.

The Bahamas pirates became so cocksure that in 1718, when the British government sent a fleet of ships to clear the islands of piracy, one of them – Charles Vane – sailed down the line of naval vessels saluting each one.

That same year, however, a new governor arrived who at last succeeded in clearing the Bahamas of pirates. He was Woodes Rogers, originally a merchant from Bristol, and himself a former pirate. Between 1708 and 1711, Rogers made a privateering voyage to make up for the losses he had suffered when pirates seized his ships. Rogers looted the Spanish colony at Guayaquil, Ecuador, where he stole a fortune in silver and valuables. On his way home to England he captured a Spanish galleon with treasure on board worth £1 million.

As governor, Rogers dealt with the Bahamas pirates by first offering them a pardon. Some accepted. Those who did not were very severely dealt with. In November 1718 Rogers had three captured pirates put on trial, followed by ten more in December.

From then on the 2,000 pirates still at large in the Caribbean avoided the Bahamas. As for Charles Vane, he accepted the pardon Rogers offered, but wanted to keep all his ill-gotten gains. When Rogers refused, Vane hoisted the Jolly Roger, fired one last defiant salvo, and sailed away. He was never seen in the Bahamas again.

From *World History* by Brenda Ralph Lewis

What heading would you give this passage?

....

What subheadings would you give paragraph 2 and 3?

....

Now summarise (write a shortened version of) this extract. Use a separate sheet of paper, and try to write no more than 80 words. Here are some guidelines to help you.

- Read the first sentence, think about it, then read the last sentence. Then read the whole piece carefully, thinking about the facts.
- Note down the main points, leaving out the examples and unimportant information.
- Write the summary from your notes (not from the original text); your writing should make sense on its own. If you have less than 70 words, you might have left out something important.

Dictionary work

List the words below in **alphabetical order**. Look up the words in your dictionary to find their meanings, uses and origins. Continue on page 11. D

immediately conscience apparent embarrass sincerely

recommend correspond thorough disastrous sufficient

opportunity mischievous committee

.... meanings: ....
uses: ....
origins: ....

.... meanings: ....
uses: ....
origins: ....

.... meanings: ....
uses: ....
origins: ....

.... meanings: ....
uses: ....
origins: ....

.... meanings: ....
uses: ....
origins: ....

.... meanings: ....
uses: ....
origins: ....

.... meanings: ....
uses: ....
origins: ....

.... meanings: ....
uses: ....
origins: ....

.... meanings: ....
uses: ....
origins: ....

.... meanings: ....
uses: ....
origins: ....

.... meanings: ....
uses: ....
origins: ....

.... meanings: ....
uses: ....
origins: ....

.... meanings: ....
uses: ....
origins: ....

Sentence-building

Simple sentences can be made longer by adding **clauses**. A **compound sentence** consists of two or more clauses of equal importance. A **complex sentence** consists of one or more main clauses and another clause that needs the others to make complete sense.

Jack heard a strange noise. (**simple sentence** – one clause)

Jack heard a strange noise, and we were scared. (**compound sentence** – two simple sentences joined by **and** to make two equally important clauses)

Jack heard a strange noise, and we were scared when he told us about it. (**complex sentence** – there is a third clause, which needs the others to make complete sense.)

Build these **simple sentences** into **compound sentences** by adding a clause of equal importance. The first one has been done for you.
Remember: A **clause** is a group of words that includes a verb.

The dog barked.

The dog barked, but we didn't hear anything.

The rain fell.

....

She ran across the park.

....

The computer crashed.

....

Now build your **compound sentences** into **complex sentences** by adding another clause.

The dog barked, but we didn't hear anything
because the television was too loud.

....

....

....

....

Different types of writing

The text extracts below could have come from any of the following types of writing: **instructions**, **explanations**, **poems**, **folk tales**, **novels**, **information** or **arguments**. Read each extract, then decide which type of writing it is.

Stop! Before you throw anything away, think ... .

The old miller knew he had not long to live so ... .

If the water is added gradually to the powder in the test tube, then ... .

Thus, the water evaporates and returns to the atmosphere. ....

That peculiar person from Putney! ....

The day was warm, though cloudy,
and I noticed a strange scent in the air ... .

a blue-grey day
a Saturday ....

Surely you must realise that ... .

Add the beaten egg ... .

The second planet from the Sun is called ... .

Choose one of the above extracts that comes from a **fiction** book. Imagine what the rest of the paragraph might look like, and write a draft version on a separate sheet of paper. Then write the finished paragraph below.
Remember: **Fiction** means text that was invented by the writer.

....

....

....

....

If you want to, do the same thing by choosing an extract from a **non-fiction** book. Write the paragraph on a separate sheet of paper.
Remember: **Non-fiction** means that the information in the piece of writing is factual.

Comparing poems

Read these two **poems** aloud, listening to the **rhythms** and the **sounds**.

1
I Am the Rain

I am the rain
I like to play games
like sometimes
        I pretend
I'm going
        to fall
Man that's the time
I don't come at all
Like sometimes
I get these laughing stitches
up my sides
        rushing people in
and out
        with the clothesline
I just love drip
        dropping
down collars
        and spines
Maybe it's a shame
but it's the only way
I get some fame

Grace Nichols

2
Sky

Tall and blue
true and open

So open my arms have room
for all the world
for sun and moon
        for birds and stars

Yet how I wish I had the chance
to come drifting down to earth –
        a simple bed sheet
covering some little girl or boy
just for a night
        but I am Sky
        that's why

Grace Nichols

Can you find some pairs of **half-rhymes** in these poems? List them below.
Remember: **Half-rhymes** are words that nearly rhyme. For example: pan/pun, wreck/rack.

Poem 1 ....

Poem 2 ....

Read the **poems** again, listening to the **beat** and the **rhythm**. Are they the same in both poems?

....

Can you find any repeated **vowel sounds** in the **poems**? If so, write them below.
Remember: The letters **a**, **e**, **i**, **o** and **u** are **vowels**. The letter **y** is sometimes also a **vowel**.

Poem 1 ....

Poem 2 ....

Investigating poems

Reread the **poems** on page 14. What do you notice about the **punctuation** in both poems?

....

....

What do you notice about the way the poems are **set out**? Look where the lines start.

....

....

Who or what is speaking in poem 1?

....

Who or what is speaking in poem 2?

....

Can these poems be placed under the same heading? If so, what might that heading be?

....

What evidence is there that *Sky* and *I Am the Rain* were written by the same **poet**? Answer this question by writing a **paragraph**; use some of your answers to the questions above, and any other similarities you may have noticed.

....

....

....

....

....

....

....

....

....

Fast fact-finding

Read the passage below.

Sky Colours

HAVE YOU EVER WONDERED why clear skies are sometimes deep blue and at other times almost white? Or why some sunsets are fiery red and others watery yellow? The reason is that the mixture of particles in the atmosphere is constantly changing. Every colour in the sky comes from the Sun. Sunlight is white, which means it is a mix of every colour in the rainbow. But as it passes through the atmosphere, gases, dust, ice crystals and water droplets split it into the various colours, bouncing some towards our eyes and absorbing others. The colours we see depend on which colours are reflected and which are absorbed. Clear skies are blue because gases in the air reflect mostly blue light from the Sun. The sky gets paler when extra dust or moisture reflects other colours, diluting the blue. Sunsets are yellow (or red, if the air is dusty) because the Sun's rays have to travel so far through the lower atmosphere that all the yellow light is absorbed.

From *How the Earth Works* by John Farndon

Underline all the **main points** in the paragraph above. Then answer these questions in full sentences.

What colour is sunlight?

....

Why is the sky blue?

....

....

What do you notice about the first four words? Why do you think they are set out this way?

....

....

What kind of sentences introduce the passage?

....

....

Words such as **the reason is, because** and **which means** tell us that this piece of writing does more than simply list facts. What else does it do?

....

....

Following instructions

Read the following piece of writing.

Experiment: Red and Blue Skies

It is not always easy to believe that all the colours in the sky come from the different way particles in the atmosphere reflect and absorb sunlight. But you can demonstrate it for yourself with this very simple experiment. The effects are quite subtle, and not always easy to see, so you need to conduct the experiment in a very dark room. Fill a straight glass with cold water, then add half a teaspoonful of milk. Now try shining the torch at the glass from different angles and watch how the colour of the milky water changes very slightly. Hold the torch close to the glass for a better effect. Add another half-teaspoonful of milk and repeat. Finally, add a full teaspoonful of milk, and try shining the torch at the glass from a variety of different angles.

From *How the Earth Works* by John Farndon

Read through the text again, underlining the actual **instructions**. On a separate sheet of paper, draw a **flow chart** that shows the **instructions** in the correct order.

Try the **experiment** yourself, then make **notes** under these headings.

Equipment/materials needed ....

....

What I did ....

....

....

What I saw ....

....

What I learnt from the experiment ....

....

....

Reporting

Write a brief factual **report** on the experiment featured on page 17.
Remember: Use straightforward statements in the passive voice when writing a **report**. For example, write **the milk is mixed with the water** rather than **I mixed the milk with the water**.

....

....

....

....

....

....

....

....

....

Do you think this old **saying** is likely to be true?

Red sky at night, shepherd's delight –
Red sky in the morning, shepherd's warning.

....

....

In your own words, write an **explanation** of why the sky appears to change colour and what causes this. Before you write, try to find out more information. Use **reference books**, **CD-ROMs** or the **Internet**. Then compare your findings with the information on page 16. Don't forget to say where you got your information from. Begin here, and continue on a separate sheet of paper.

....

....

....

....

....

....

Paragraphs and punctuation

Rewrite the following passage in **paragraphs**, **punctuating** it and changing small letters into capital letters where necessary.
Remember: **Paragraphs** separate ideas, themes or instructions. Without paragraphs, writing can be difficult to understand.

rainbows

my heart leaps up when i behold a rainbow in the sky wrote william wordsworth the famous poet and most of us share his feelings when we are lucky enough to see a rainbow there is an old saying that a pot of gold is buried at the end of the rainbow but have you ever tried to reach a rainbows end of course its impossible because a rainbow is really just the result of the raindrops refracting and reflecting light from our sun there are seven colours in the rainbow red orange yellow green blue indigo and violet

Rewrite this section of a **play script** as a **story**. Use **paragraphs** and **speech marks**. Write on a separate sheet of paper, and continue the story, if you wish.
Remember: When writing **direct speech** (dialogue), start a new paragraph each time the speaker changes.

NICK: It's raining again, but the sun is shining as well.
SOPHIE: I think we should go swimming anyway.
NICK: We might get wet … let's wait a bit longer.
SOPHIE: We can't swim without getting wet, Nick. What difference does it make?
NICK: Hey!
SOPHIE: What is it?
NICK: Look – a rainbow over the beach!
SOPHIE: Quick, get your spade – we'll be rich!

Old text

Read this **extract** carefully, then answer, in full sentences, the questions that follow.

For some minutes Alice stood without speaking, looking out in all directions over the country – and a most curious country it was. There were a number of tiny little brooks running straight across it from side to side, and the ground between was divided up into squares by a number of little green hedges, that reached from brook to brook.

"I declare it's marked out just like a large chess-board!" Alice said at last. "There ought to be some men moving about somewhere – and so there are!" she added in a tone of delight, and her heart began to beat quick with excitement as she went on. "It's a great huge game of chess that's being played – all over the world – if this *is* the world at all, you know. Oh, what fun it is! How I *wish* I was one of them! I wouldn't mind being a Pawn, if only I might join – though of course I should *like* to be a Queen, best."

She glanced rather shyly at the real Queen as she said this, but her companion only smiled pleasantly, and said "That's easily managed. You can be the White Queen's Pawn, if you like, as Lily's too young to play; and you're in the Second Square to begin with: when you get to the Eighth Square you'll be a Queen –" Just at this moment, somehow or other, they began to run.

From *Through the Looking Glass* by Lewis Carroll

Who is the **main character** in this story?

....

Where is this episode **set**? Describe the **setting** in your own words.

....

....

Does Alice expect to enjoy this part of her adventure or not? How can you tell?

....

....

Why would Alice rather be a queen than a pawn?

....

What chess piece would you want to be, and why?

....

....

Can you find any words or phrases to suggest that this was written a long time ago?

....

....

New text

Read this **extract** carefully, then answer in full sentences, the questions that follow.

They followed, running again. Once inside the house, with its maze of corridors, they could lose her. But there she was – they heard her first, those dragging footsteps. Then, hurrying, they saw her blue cloak, fair head. She pushed a huge panelled door and passed through, leaving it open behind her. They reached it and peered in just in time to see Sarah passing through yet another door on the far side of a room that was evidently part of the main house. There was heavy, gleaming furniture, walls lined with gilt-framed pictures, richly draped windows. Minty set off across it …

They were through the second door now, and into an amazing crimson. 'Cor!' Tom was awestruck. 'Red Drawing Room, this is! Heard about it! Cor! Ain't it just red?'

It was. Carpet, walls, hangings smouldered, blazed. The very air breathed red.

Sarah had vanished. Minty crossed the room and came into a vast light entrance hall. There, on the great black and white diamonds of the floor, was that small blue figure, a chess piece.

At that moment there came other footsteps, a clatter and rattle. Sarah stopped in her tracks, Minty and Tom stiffened.

From *Moondial* by Helen Cresswell

Where is this episode set? Describe the setting in your own words.

....

....

Name the three characters and write a word to describe what each one is thinking.

....

....

Why do you think Sarah is described as "a chess piece"?

....

....

Pick a descriptive phrase and explain the effect it creates for the reader.

....

....

Is the next part of this story likely to be funny or threatening? How can you tell?

....

....

Is this extract more modern than the extract on page 20? Give reasons for your answer.

....

....

Comparing texts

Use the following questions to help you **plan** a **comparison** of the **extracts** on pages 20 and 21.

Underline the words of the **narrator** in both extracts. Write a sentence comparing them.

....

....

Draw a ring around the **conversations** in both extracts. What differences can you see?

....

....

Compare the **styles** of the two authors (their particular way of writing).

....

....

Which of these terms could be used for the stories: **traditional**, **fantasy**, **novel**, **adventure**, **autobiography**, **romance**, **historical**? Explain your answer.

....

....

Would you like to read more of either of these books? Which one and why?

....

....

Describe a dramatic experience in the style of either writer.
Remember to use **paragraphs**.
Begin here, and continue on a separate sheet of paper.

....

....

....

....

....

....

....

Reported speech

Rewrite the following text in **reported speech**. It has been started for you. Continue on a separate sheet of paper if necessary.
Remember: **Reported speech** reports what the characters have said, rather than quoting their actual words. **Reported speech** is in the **past tense** and has no speech marks.

The Queen propped her up against a tree, and said kindly, "You may rest a little, now."

Alice looked round her in great surprise. "Why, I do believe we've been under this tree the whole time! Everything's just as it was!"

"Of course it is," said the Queen: "what would you have it?"

"Well, in *our* country," said Alice, still panting a little, "you'd generally get to somewhere else – if you ran very fast for a long time, as we've been doing."

"A slow sort of country!" said the Queen. "Now, *here*, you see, it takes all the running *you* can do, to keep in the same place. If you want to get somewhere else, you must run at least twice as fast as that!"

"I'd rather not try, please!" said Alice. "I'm quite content to stay here – only I *am* so hot and thirsty!"

"I know what *you'd* like!" the Queen said good-naturedly, taking a little box out of her pocket. "Have a biscuit?"

From *Through the Looking Glass* by Lewis Carroll

The Queen propped her up against a tree and told her kindly that she ....

....

....

....

....

....

....

....

....

....

....

Most authors use a mixture of **reported** and **direct speech**. Why do you think they do this?

....

....

Character development

Reread the extracts on pages 20 and 23.

What are the good qualities about the Red Queen?

....

What are the bad qualities about the Red Queen?

....

Read this extract from a later chapter.

Everything was happening so oddly that she didn't feel a bit surprised at finding the Red Queen and the White Queen sitting close to her, one on each side: she would have liked very much to ask them how they came there, but she feared it would not be quite civil. However, there would be no harm, she thought, in asking if the game was over. "Please, would you tell me – " she began, looking timidly at the Red Queen.

"Speak when you're spoken to!" the Queen sharply interrupted her.

"But if everybody obeyed that rule," said Alice, who was always ready for a little argument, "and if you only spoke when you were spoken to, and the other person always waited for *you* to begin, you see nobody would ever say anything, so that – "
"Ridiculous!" cried the Queen. "Why, don't you see, child –" here she broke off with a frown, and, after thinking for a minute, suddenly changed the subject of the conversation. "What do you mean by 'If you really are a Queen'? What right have you to all yourself so? You can't be a Queen, you know, till you've passed the proper examination. And the sooner we begin it, the better."

From *Through the Looking Glass* by Lewis Carroll

What qualities does the Red Queen have in this extract?

....

....

If you met the Red Queen what would you like to ask her?

....

....

At the end of the book, the Red Queen changes into Alice's pet kitten.
Why may the Red Queen be like a kitten?

....

....

Introducing characters

Pirates feature in many popular stories. Pirate characters have also appeared on stage, in film and on television. Now it is your turn to create a script with pirates as the main characters.
This planning sheet will help you to get started. Make brief notes only.

Setting – time and place (Will the scene take place in the past, present or future? Is it set on Earth or elsewhere?)

....

....

Characters – about three or four only (Who are your characters? What are their good and bad qualities? How will you interest your audience in them?)

....

....

....

....

Plot – what happens (What events or actions take place? How do the characters react to these events?)

....

....

....

....

....

....

Write your script on a separate sheet of paper. Before you write, you will need to have a clear idea of what happens at the beginning and end of your scene. Also remember to give directions for the camera and for the characters actions. Write the dialogue next to the characters names (without speech marks).

A questionnaire

Complete this brief **questionnaire** about your reading.

Fiction

Tick the types of **fiction** that you enjoy reading.

novels ☐ short stories ☐ science fiction ☐ historical ☐

adventure ☐ mystery ☐ fantasy ☐ others ....

My favourite **authors** are ....

My favourite **fiction** titles are ....

....

Poetry

Tick the types of **poems** that you enjoy.

ballads ☐ haiku ☐ cinquain ☐ free verse ☐

limericks ☐ shape poems ☐ others ....

My favourite **poets** are ....

My favourite **poems** are ....

....

Non-fiction

Tick the types of **non-fiction** that you enjoy reading.

sports ☐ games ☐ hobbies ☐ animal care ☐ computers ☐

science ☐ art ☐ music ☐ TV, film, etc. ☐ others ....

My favourite **non-fiction** titles are ....

....

Now write more about your favourite types of reading on a separate sheet of paper. Try to persuade other people of your age to read the books or poems that you enjoy the most. Take care with your **punctuation**, **spelling** and **handwriting**.

Prefixes

Read the following list of **prefixes,** then write the **prefixes** in **alphabetical order**.
Remember: A **prefix** is a group of letters added to the beginning of a word to change its meaning.

post- ante- kilo- pro- geo- bio- retro- vari- zoo- multi-
hydro- sub- extra- ultra- fore- peri- iso- contra- thermo-

Use a **dictionary** to find a word beginning with each of the **prefixes** listed above. Write each word in a sentence that shows its meaning. D

antechamber: We came to a small antechamber before entering the main hall.

Suffixes

Follow the instructions below for each of the words in this list.

artist	importance	stationary	changeable	lioness
sorrowful	telegraph	clarify	advertise	magnetism
senseless	skilfully	happiness	headship	attitude
motion	cruelty	otherwise	pomposity	

1 Write the word in the first column of the **chart**.
2 Decide which part of the word is its **suffix**, and write it in the second column.
3 Think of another word with the same **suffix**, and check its spelling in a dictionary. D
4 Write the new word in the third column of the **chart**.

Remember: A **suffix** is a group of letters added to the end of a word to change its meaning.

artist	-ist	chemist

Joining sentences

The **sentences** below are about the game of chess, but they are in the wrong order. Read through the **sentences** and decide on the best order.

Computers play chess. Chess remains popular today. There are sixteen pieces on each side. Chess is a game for two people. "Checkmate" means that the king cannot move without being taken by another piece. The board and the pieces can be in any two contrasting colours. Pieces move in different ways. Computers sometimes beat human champions. Chess is played on a chequered board. It seems complicated at first. Each side has one king, one queen, two knights, two bishops, two rooks and eight pawns. The board is usually black and white. The game ends when one of the kings is "checkmated". Experts improve their game by learning special patterns of moves. Chess is a very old game.

Write the sentences in order here.

1 ....

2 ....

3 ....

4 ....

5 ....

6 ....

7 ....

8 ....

9 ....

10 ....

11 ....

12 ....

13 ....

14 ....

15 ....

All these **sentences** about chess are very short. **Join** some of the **sentences** to make the piece of writing read more fluently. You may need to add, remove or change some words, but make sure you keep all the main ideas. Write out your **sentences** on a separate sheet of paper.

Active and passive

Active sentences describe an action done **by the subject.**

I directed the award-winning film. (an **active** sentence)

Passive sentences describe an action done **to the subject.**

The award-winning film was directed by me. (a **passive** sentence)

Change these sentences from **passive** to **active**.

The match was won by our team.

Our team ....

The winning goal was scored by Rachel.

....

The party was enjoyed by all my friends.

....

Jack was stung by an unusual insect.

....

Now change these sentences from **active** to **passive**.

Aliens invade our planet.

Our planet is ....

Leonardo da Vinci painted the *Mona Lisa.*

....

The team dislike the group leader.

....

The hero piloted his craft with great skill.

....

A hurricane struck the town.

....

Colons, semicolons and dashes

Punctuation can be used to connect groups of words. The **punctuation marks** that do this are: the **colon (:)**, the **semicolon (;)** and the **dash (–)**.

Read each sentence below, and write another sentence using the same **punctuation marks**.
Remember:

- A **colon** is used to introduce a list, a quotation or a second clause that makes the first clause easier to understand. (A clause is a group of words with a verb in it.)
- A **semicolon** is used to link complete clauses that are too closely related to separate with a full stop.
  It can also be used to separate items in a list that already has commas in it.
- A **dash** can be used to separate a comment from the rest of a sentence. It makes a stronger break than a comma and is less formal than brackets.

Bring these things with you**:** a jumper, your swimsuit, your lunch and your bus fare.

....

....

It was Shakespeare's Juliet who asked**:** "What's in a name?"

....

The match was abandoned**:** rain poured down.

....

....

We had to stop playing**;** I went to Matt's house.

....

I bought a kilo of big, juicy apples**;** two large, ripe lemons**;** a grapefruit and a punnet of delicious, sweet-smelling strawberries.

....

....

....

The weather is lovely **–** wish you were here!

....

Word search

Find the 12 words below in the word search.

p	a	v	e	r	a	g	e	l	c
r	v	c	a	q	u	e	u	e	o
o	a	e	c	p	s	r	o	i	m
g	r	s	h	o	y	a	m	s	m
r	i	o	i	e	m	s	m	u	u
a	e	c	e	h	b	p	e	r	n
m	t	c	v	p	o	v	a	e	i
m	y	u	e	y	l	o	s	n	t
e	s	p	e	c	i	a	l	l	y
s	s	y	s	t	e	m	e	y	n

Learn these words.

programme   especially   community   accompany   symbol   achieve

average   variety   occupy   leisure   queue   system

Choose six words. Write a sentence for each one to show its meaning. D

Answer Section with Parents' Notes

Key Stage 2
Ages 10–11

This 8-page section provides answers or explanatory notes to all the activities in this book. This will enable you to assess your child's work.

Point out any spelling mistakes, incorrect punctuation and grammatical errors as you mark each page. Also correct any handwriting errors. (Your child should use the handwriting style taught at his or her school.) As well as making corrections, it is very important to praise your child's efforts and achievements.

Encourage your child to use a dictionary, and suggest that he or she uses a notebook to compile a **word bank** of new words or difficult spellings.

2

Riddles

Can you solve this word-building **riddle**?

My first is in **bread** but not in **bead**.
My second is in **dig** but not in **dug**.
My third is in **fled** but not in **flew**.
My fourth is in **hid** but not in **hit**.
My fifth is in **held** but not in **herd**.
My sixth is in **step** but not in **stop**.

Answer ....riddle........

Now try this one.

My first is in **bite** but not in **site**.
My second is in **tent** but not in **tint**.
My third is in **grow** but not in **brow**.
My fourth is in **in** but not in **on**.
My fifth is in **ton** but not in **tow**.
My sixth is in **stone** but not in **store**.
My seventh is in **pin** but not in **pun**.
My eighth is in **naught** but not in **caught**.
My ninth is in **grip** but not in **drip**.

Answer ....beginning........

Try to make some word-building **riddles** of your own. Choose from the list of words below. The first one has been started for you. Continue your **riddles** on an extra sheet of paper.

business	colonel	family	friend	height	necessary
immediate	medicine	neighbour	occasion	queue	rhythm
separate	skilful	twelfth	weird	yacht	

My first is in **bite** but not in **mite**.
My second is in **cup** but not in **cap**.
My third is in **sew** but not in **dew**.
My fourth is in **in** but not in **an**.
My fifth is in **ton** but not in **toe**.

My sixth is in .... but not in ....
My seventh is in .... but not in ....
My eighth is in .... but not in ....

Answers may vary

These activities, based on riddles, help draw your child's attention to the spelling of some common words that are often misspelt. The formula for these riddles can be reversed if it helps. For example: My first is in *first* and also in *fourth*.

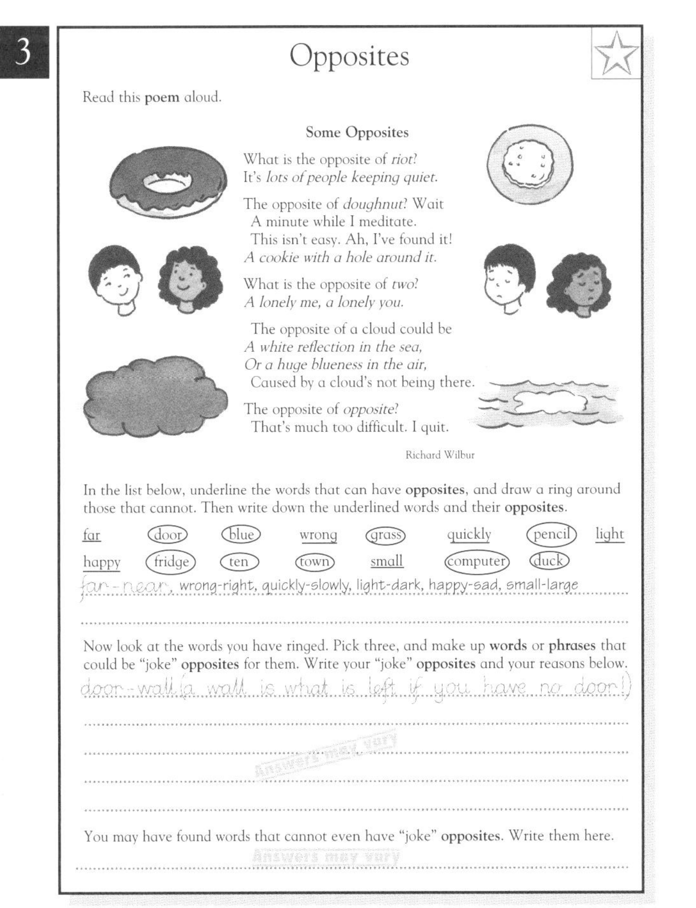

3

Opposites

Read this **poem** aloud.

Some Opposites

What is the opposite of *riot*?
It's *lots of people keeping quiet*.

The opposite of *doughnut*? Wait
A minute while I meditate.
This isn't easy. Ah, I've found it!
A cookie with a hole around it.

What is the opposite of *two*?
A lonely me, a lonely you.

The opposite of a cloud could be
A white reflection in the sea,
Or a huge blueness in the air,
Caused by a cloud's not being there.

The opposite of *opposite*?
That's much too difficult. I quit.

Richard Wilbur

In the list below, underline the words that can have **opposites**, and draw a ring around those that cannot. Then write down the underlined words and their **opposites**.

far (door) (blue) wrong (grass) quickly (pencil) light
happy (fridge) (ten) (town) small (computer) (duck)

far-near, wrong-right, quickly-slowly, light-dark, happy-sad, small-large

Now look at the words you have ringed. Pick three, and make up **words** or **phrases** that could be "joke" **opposites** for them. Write your "joke" **opposites** and your reasons below.

door-wall (a wall is what is left if you have no door!)

Answers may vary

You may have found words that cannot even have "joke" **opposites**. Write them here.

Answers may vary

The activities on this page focus on opposites. If your child comes up with justifiable opposites that are not included here, you could discuss the validity of the concept of opposites (which is the theme of the poem).

4

Spoonerisms

Kinquering congs is a well-known example of a **spoonerism**. W. A. Spooner from Oxford, England, accidentally "invented" **spoonerisms**: he often mixed up the sounds at the beginning of his words.

What did W. A. Spooner mean to say instead of kinquering congs?

Conquering kings

Here are some modern **spoonerisms** for you to "translate" into English – take care with the spelling!

Did you hear the roar-bell ding?

Did you hear the doorbell ring?

Don't forget to dock the law!

Don't forget to lock the door!

We had thick frog last fiday.

We had thick fog last Friday.

Do you like to bead in red?

Do you like to read in bed?

I can fee my sootprints!

I can see my footprints!

I caught a ban of lemon drink.

I bought a can of lemon drink.

Can you think of any **spoonerisms** yourself? Write them here.

Answers may vary

This page introduces your child to a fun way of playing with sounds and spellings – the spoonerism. Help your child to use a dictionary to check any words that he or she cannot spell.

5 Malapropisms

Mrs. Malaprop is a character in a play by R. B. Sheridan. She often gets her words mixed up, using a word that sounds almost, but not quite, like the correct one. For instance, she says the word **allegory** when she means to say **alligator!**

Look up the word **allegory** in the dictionary, then explain the obvious difference between **allegory** and **alligator**.

Answers may vary

Here are some **malapropisms** for you to correct – draw a ring around the word that is used incorrectly, then rewrite the sentence using the correct word.

There are three (angels) in a triangle.
There are three angles in the triangle.

We decided to sign the (partition).
We decided to sign the petition.

I am pleased to (except) this prize.
I am pleased to accept this prize.

The brakes on a bike work by (fraction).
The brakes on a bike work by friction.

The (jugular) prepared to pounce.
The jaguar prepared to pounce.

Now find the meanings of the words you ringed, and write them here.

Answers may vary

These exercises provide practice with words that sound similar but are spelt differently. Again, it may be helpful for your child to use a dictionary to check the spellings or meanings of words. Remember to praise correct answers.

6 More malapropisms

The character Dogberry is a Watchman (like a policeman) in Shakespeare's play *Much Ado About Nothing*. He is a memorable comic character because he uses malapropisms in his speech.

Here are some lines from Act III Scene 5.
Underline in Dogberry's lines below the six malapropisms he uses.

LEONATO: What would you with me, honest neighbour?

DOGBERRY: Marry, sir, I would have some confidence with you that decerns you nearly.

LEONATO: Brief, I pray you, for you see it is a busy time with me.

DOGBERRY: Yea, an't 'twere a thousand pound more than 'tis, for I hear as good exclamation on your worship as of any man in the city; and though I be but a poor man, I am glad to hear it.

LEONATO: I would fain know what you have to say.

DOGBERRY: One word, sir: our watch, sir, have indeed comprehended two aspicious persons, and we would have them this morning examined before your worship.

LEONATO: Take their examination yourself and bring it me; I am now in great haste, as it may appear unto you.

DOGBERRY: It shall be suffigance.

Write the meanings of these words that Dogberry meant to use.

conference

concern

acclamation

apprehended

suspicious

sufficient

Answers may vary

Your child may be studying one or more of Shakespeare's plays at school. If your child is finding it difficult to find the malapropism then encourage them to look at the words in the second part that Dogberry meant to use.

7 Words that confuse

In the piece of writing below, many words sound right but are spelt incorrectly – the wrong homophone has been used. Read through the passage, underlining each wrong word. Then rewrite the passage with the correct spellings.

Could I survive on a desert aisle? I wood make a hut on the beech from steaks and bits of would. Their would knot bee thyme to get board. I mite try in vein two escape, waiving at plains or passing ships. My hare would grow long. I might have to sow up a peace of sale from my wrecked boat to make knew clothes – a reel site four saw eyes!

Could I survive on a desert isle? I would make a hut on the beach from stakes and bits of wood. There would not be time to get bored. I might try in vain to escape, waving at planes or passing ships. My hair would grow long. I might have to sew up a piece of sail from my wrecked boat to make new clothes – a real sight for sore eyes!

The following words are often confused. Write a sentence to show the meaning for each word.

affect

effect

eligible

illegible

cereal

serial

compliment

complement

Answers may vary

The exercises on this page provide practice in selecting the correct homophone in context and in spotting spelling errors. If your child is in doubt about how a word should be spelt, encourage him or her to check the word in a dictionary.

8 Inventing words

Use a **dictionary** to complete these **definitions**.

A micro chip is a very small chip of silicone.

A microprocessor is a part of computer that controls the funtions of the computer's central processing unit.

A microclimate is the climate of a very small area.

A micro-organism is a very small living thing.

An instrument used to look at very small objects is a microscope .

Find three more words beginning with the **prefix** micro- and explain their meanings.

A micro .... is ....

A micro .... is ....

A micro .... is ....

Answers may vary

Now make up some new "micro" words, and **define** them. For example, a microsnack is a snack that is too small to be satisfying but too tasty to resist.

Answers may vary

Complete these **definitions**.

A mega byte is a very large unit of computer memory.

A megaphone is a funnel-shaped device that makes a voice sound louder.

A megamouth is a shark with a very large mouth.

A megalopolis is a very large city or urban area.

A megalith is a very large stone or rock.

Now make up some "mega" words, and **define** them. For example, a megamouse is an extra-large mouse from the planet Megary.

Answers may vary

On this page, your child experiments with inventing and building words. You could extend this idea by asking your child to think up a word game based on invented words or to write a dictionary of invented words.

9

Information text

Although pirates in stories are often portrayed as lovable rogues, the real-life pirates who sailed the oceans searching out laden ships were usually ruthless robbers. Read the following historical information about real pirates.

The Bahamas pirates became so cocksure that in 1718, when the British government sent a fleet of ships to clear the islands of piracy, one of them – Charles Vane – sailed down the line of naval vessels saluting each one.

That same year, however, a new governor arrived who at last succeeded in clearing the Bahamas of pirates. He was Woodes Rogers, originally a merchant from Bristol, and himself a former pirate. Between 1708 and 1711, Rogers made a privateering voyage to make up for the losses he had suffered when pirates seized his ships. Rogers looted the Spanish colony at Guayaquil, Ecuador, where he stole a fortune in silver and valuables. On his way home to England he captured a Spanish galleon with treasure on board worth £1 million.

As governor, Rogers dealt with the Bahamas pirates by first offering them a pardon. Some accepted. Those who did not were very severely dealt with. In November 1718 Rogers had three captured pirates put on trial, followed by ten more in December.

From then on the 2,000 pirates still at large in the Caribbean avoided the Bahamas. As for Charles Vane, he accepted the pardon Rogers offered, but wanted to keep all his ill-gotten gains. When Rogers refused, Vane hoisted the Jolly Roger, fired one last defiant salvo, and sailed away. He was never seen in the Bahamas again.

From *World History* by Brenda Ralph Lewis

What heading would you give this passage?

Answers may vary

What subheadings would you give paragraph 2 and 3?

Answers may vary

Now summarise (write a shortened version of) this extract. Use a separate sheet of paper, and try to write no more than 80 words. Here are some guidelines to help you.

- Read the first sentence, think about it, then read the last sentence. Then read the whole piece carefully, thinking about the facts.
- Note down the main points, leaving out the examples and unimportant information.
- Write the summary from your notes (not from the original text); your writing should make sense on its own. If you have less than 70 words, you might have left out something important.

Here your child learns to summarise a piece of text in a specified number of words. Your child's summary needs to include all the main points from the passage and to make sense on its own. Help your child to follow the guidelines.

10

Dictionary work

List the words below in **alphabetical order**. Look up the words in your dictionary to find their meanings, uses and origins. Continue on page 11. D

immediately conscience apparent embarrass sincerely
recommend correspond thorough disastrous sufficient
opportunity mischievous committee

apparent meanings: uses: origins:

committee meanings: uses: origins:

conscience meanings: uses: origins:

correspond meanings: uses: origins:

disastrous meanings: uses: origins:

Answers may vary

The exercise on pages 10 and 11 provides dictionary practice. Take this chance to look at a dictionary with your child. It may help if you explain the parts of an entry, discussing plurals, pronunciation guides, abbreviations and definitions.

11

embarrass meanings: uses: origins:

immediately meanings: uses: origins:

mischievous meanings: uses: origins:

opportunity meanings: uses: origins:

recommend meanings: uses: origins:

sincerely meanings: uses: origins:

sufficient meanings: uses: origins:

thorough meanings: uses: origins:

Answers may vary

Look at the alphabetical order in a dictionary with your child. Talk about how it lists words that start with the same letter, then uses the second, third or fourth letter of each word to decide which word appears first.

12

Sentence-building

Simple sentences can be made longer by adding **clauses**. A **compound sentence** consists of two or more clauses of equal importance. A **complex sentence** consists of one or more main clauses and another clause that needs the others to make complete sense.

Jack heard a strange noise. (**simple sentence** – one clause)

Jack heard a strange noise, and we were scared. (**compound sentence** – two simple sentences joined by **and** to make two equally important clauses)

Jack heard a strange noise, and we were scared when he told us about it. (**complex sentence** – there is a third clause, which needs the others to make complete sense.)

Build these **simple sentences** into **compound sentences** by adding a clause of equal importance. The first one has been done for you.
Remember: A **clause** is a group of words that includes a verb.

The dog barked.

The dog barked, but we didn't hear anything.

The rain fell.

She ran across the park.

The computer crashed.

Now build your **compound sentences** into **complex sentences** by adding another clause.

The dog barked, but we didn't hear anything because the television was too loud.

Answers may vary

On this page your child learns how sentences can be made longer by the addition of clauses. Check that your child understands the examples on this page, particularly the point that every clause must contain a verb.

13

Different types of writing

The text extracts below could have come from any of the following types of writing: **instructions, explanations, poems, folk tales, novels, information** or **arguments**. Read each extract, then decide which type of writing it is.

Stop! Before you throw anything away, think ...	instruction
The old miller knew he had not long to live so ...	folktale
If the water is added gradually to the powder in the test tube, then ...	information
Thus, the water evaporates and returns to the atmosphere.	explanation
That peculiar person from Putney!	poem
The day was warm, though cloudy, and I noticed a strange scent in the air ...	novel
a blue-grey day a Saturday	poem
Surely you must realise that ...	argument
Add the beaten egg...	instruction
The second planet from the Sun is called ...	information

Choose one of the above extracts that comes from a **fiction** book. Imagine what the rest of the paragraph might look like, and write a draft version on a separate sheet of paper. Then write the finished paragraph below.
Remember: Fiction means text that was invented by the writer.

Answers may vary

If you want to, do the same thing by choosing an extract from a **non-fiction** book. Write the paragraph on a separate sheet of paper.
Remember: Non-fiction means that the information in the piece of writing is factual.

This page helps your child to recognise the features of different genres (types) of text, and to use them in his or her own writing. Your child's paragraph should display elements of a particular style of fiction or non-fiction writing.

14

Comparing poems

Read these two **poems** aloud, listening to the **rhythms** and the **sounds**.

1
I Am the Rain

I am the rain
I like to play games
like sometimes
 I pretend
I'm going
 to fall
Man that's the time
I don't come at all
Like sometimes
I get these laughing stitches
up my sides
 rushing people in
and out
 with the clothesline
I just love drip
 dropping
down collars
 and spines
Maybe it's a shame
but it's the only way
I get some fame

Grace Nichols

2
Sky

Tall and blue
true and open

So open my arms have room
for all the world
for sun and moon
 for birds and stars

Yet how I wish I had the chance
to come drifting down to earth –
 a simple bed sheet
covering some little girl or boy
just for a night
 but I am Sky
 that's why

Grace Nichols

Can you find some pairs of **half-rhymes** in these poems? List them below.
Remember: Half-rhymes are words that nearly rhyme. For example: pan/pun, wreck/rack.

Poem 1 rain / games / clothesline / spines

Poem 2 room / moon

Read the **poems** again, listening to the **beat** and the **rhythm**. Are they the same in both poems?

Answers may vary

Can you find any repeated **vowel sounds** in the **poems**? If so, write them below.
Remember: The letters **a, e, i, o** and **u** are **vowels**. The letter **y** is sometimes also a **vowel**.

Poem 1 rain / play / games / shame / way / fame time / sides / line / spines

Poem 2 blue / true room / moon sky / why

Two modern poems on the theme of the weather are presented on this page. Encourage your child to read the poems out loud and to listen for the rhyming words.

15

Investigating poems

Reread the **poems** on page 14. What do you notice about the **punctuation** in both poems?

There is very little punctuation – mainly capital letters and apostrophes.

What do you notice about the way the poems are **set out**? Look where the lines start.

The words on some lines start midway along the line.

Who or what is speaking in poem 1?

The rain is speaking in poem 1.

Who or what is speaking in poem 2?

The sky is speaking in poem 2.

Can these poems be placed under the same heading? If so, what might that heading be?

These poems could be described as poems about things in nature.

What evidence is there that *Sky* and *I Am the Rain* were written by the same **poet**? Answer this question by writing a **paragraph**; use some of your answers to the questions above, and any other similarities you may have noticed.

Answers may vary

These exercises help your child to compare two poems by the same writer and to reveal similar techniques and themes. Talk to your child about the poet's use of personification (treating things that are not human as if they were people).

16

Fast fact-finding

Read the passage below.

Sky Colours

HAVE YOU EVER WONDERED why clear skies are sometimes deep blue and at other times almost white? Or why some sunsets are fiery red and others watery yellow? The reason is that the mixture of particles in the atmosphere is constantly changing. Every colour in the sky comes from the Sun. Sunlight is white, which means it is a mix of every colour in the rainbow. But as it passes through the atmosphere, gases, dust, ice crystals and water droplets split it into the various colours, bouncing some towards our eyes and absorbing others. The colours we see depend on which colours are reflected and which are absorbed. Clear skies are blue because gases in the air reflect mostly blue light from the Sun. The sky gets paler when extra dust or moisture reflects other colours, diluting the blue. Sunsets are yellow (or red, if the air is dusty) because the Sun's rays have to travel so far through the lower atmosphere that all the yellow light is absorbed.

From *How the Earth Works* by John Farndon

Underline all the **main points** in the paragraph above. Then answer these questions in full sentences.

What colour is sunlight?

Sunlight is white.

Why is the sky blue?

The sky is blue because gases in the air reflect mostly blue light from the Sun.

What do you notice about the first four words? Why do you think they are set out this way?

The first four words are in capital letters.

They attract the readers' attention, drawing them into the text.

What kind of sentences introduce the passage?

The passage is introduced by questions.

Words such as **the reason is, because** and **which means** tell us that this piece of writing does more than simply list facts. What else does it do?

This piece of writing also explains how and why things happen.

Here your child reads a passage of information text. The questions help your child to identify the main facts and to analyse the way in which the information is presented. Check that your child writes his or her answers in complete sentences.

17 Following instructions

Read the following piece of writing.

Experiment: Red and Blue Skies

It is not always easy to believe that all the colours in the sky come from the different way particles in the atmosphere reflect and absorb sunlight. But you can demonstrate it for yourself with this very simple experiment. The effects are quite subtle, and not always easy to see, so you need to conduct the experiment in a very dark room. Fill a straight glass with cold water, then add half a teaspoonful of milk. Now try shining the torch at the glass from different angles and watch how the colour of the milky water changes very slightly. Hold the torch close to the glass for a better effect. Add another half-teaspoonful of milk and repeat. Finally, add a full teaspoonful of milk, and try shining the torch at the glass from a variety of different angles.

From *How the Earth Works* by John Farndon

Read through the text again, underlining the actual **instructions**. On a separate sheet of paper, draw a **flow chart** that shows the **instructions** in the correct order.

Try the **experiment** yourself, then make **notes** under these headings.

Equipment/materials needed straight glass of cold water, 2 tsps milk, teaspoon, torch

What I did filled straight glass with cold water, added half a teaspoonful of milk shone torch at glass from different angles

What I saw Answers may vary

What I learnt from the experiment Answers may vary

The activities on this page and the following one focus on the instructions for a scientific experiment. The exercises are designed to give your child practice in formal writing. Encourage your child to do the actual experiment.

18 Reporting

Write a brief factual **report** on the experiment featured on page 17.
Remember: Use straightforward statements in the passive voice when writing a **report**. For example, write **the milk is mixed with the water** rather than **I mixed the milk with the water**.

Answers may vary

Do you think this old **saying** is likely to be true?

Red sky at night, shepherd's delight –
Red sky in the morning, shepherd's warning.

Answers may vary

In your own words, write an **explanation** of why the sky appears to change colour and what causes this. Before you write, try to find out more information. Use **reference books**, **CD-ROMs** or the **Internet**. Then compare your findings with the information on page 16. Don't forget to say where you got your information from. Begin here, and continue on a separate sheet of paper.

Answers may vary

Check that your child's report is written in a formal style, suitable for a science notebook and that it is expressed mainly in the passive voice. The explanation should be concise and informative and contain a list of the reference sources.

19 Paragraphs and punctuation

Rewrite the following passage in **paragraphs**, **punctuating** it and changing small letters into capital letters where necessary.
Remember: **Paragraphs** separate ideas, themes or instructions. Without paragraphs, writing can be difficult to understand.

rainbows

my heart leaps up when i behold a rainbow in the sky wrote william wordsworth the famous poet and most of us share his feelings when we are lucky enough to see a rainbow there is an old saying that a pot of gold is buried at the end of the rainbow but have you ever tried to reach a rainbows end of course its impossible because a rainbow is really just the result of the raindrops refracting and reflecting light from our sun there are seven colours in the rainbow red orange yellow green blue indigo and violet

"My heart leaps up when I behold a rainbow in the sky," wrote William Wordsworth, the famous English poet, and most of us share his feelings when we are lucky enough to see a rainbow.

There is an old saying that a pot of gold is buried at the end of the rainbow, but have you ever tried to reach a rainbow's end? Of course it's impossible, because a rainbow is really just the result of the raindrops refracting and reflecting light from our Sun.

There are seven colours in the rainbow: red, orange, yellow, green, blue, indigo and violet.

Rewrite this section of a **play script** as a **story**. Use **paragraphs** and **speech marks**. Write on a separate sheet of paper, and continue the story, if you wish.
Remember: When writing **direct speech** (dialogue), start a new paragraph each time the speaker changes.

"It's raining again, but the sun is shining as well," said Nick.
"I think we should go swimming anyway," said Sophie.
"We might get wet … let's wait a bit longer," suggested Nick.
"We can't swim without getting wet, Nick. What difference does it make?" Sophie asked.
"Hey!" exclaimed Nick.
"What is it?" asked Sophie.
"Look – a rainbow over the beach!" cried Nick.
"Quick, get your spade – we'll be rich!" exclaimed Sophie.

There are many slight variations possible in the answers to these punctuation exercises. Your child may realise that there are creative choices in the use of punctuation, but a knowledge of the basic rules should be evident in his or her writing.

20 Old text

Read this **extract** carefully, then answer, in full sentences, the questions that follow.

For some minutes Alice stood without speaking, looking out in all directions over the country – and a most curious country it was. There were a number of tiny little brooks running straight across it from side to side, and the ground between was divided up into squares by a number of little green hedges, that reached from brook to brook.
"I declare it's marked out just like a large chess-board!" Alice said at last. "There ought to be some men moving about somewhere – and so there are!" she added in a tone of delight, and her heart began to beat quick with excitement as she went on. "It's a great huge game of chess that's being played – all over the world – if this *is* the world at all, you know. Oh, what fun it is! How I *wish* I was one of them! I wouldn't mind being a Pawn, if only I might join – though of course I should *like* to be a Queen, best."
She glanced rather shyly at the real Queen as she said this, but her companion only smiled pleasantly, and said: "That's easily managed. You can be the White Queen's Pawn, if you like, as Lily's too young to play; and you're in the Second Square to begin with: when you get to the Eighth Square you'll be a Queen –" Just at this moment, somehow or other, they began to run.

From *Through the Looking Glass* by Lewis Carroll

Who is the **main character** in this story?
The main character in the story is Alice.

Where is this episode **set**? Describe the **setting** in your own words.
The episode is set in a strange country with streams and hedges forming squares like those on a chessboard.

Does Alice expect to enjoy this part of her adventure or not? How can you tell?
Yes. Alice sounds delighted and is very excited about joining in the game.

Why would Alice rather be a queen than a pawn?
The queen is far more important and powerful than a pawn.

What chess piece would you want to be, and why?
Answers may vary

Can you find any words or phrases to suggest that this was written a long time ago?
Phrases that suggest this was written a long time ago include: a most curious country it was; I declare; Oh what fun it is!; How I wish I was one of them.

On this page and the following one, your child compares two extracts from children's books. They are from different periods in time, but share a similar theme. Check that your child writes his or her answers in full sentences.

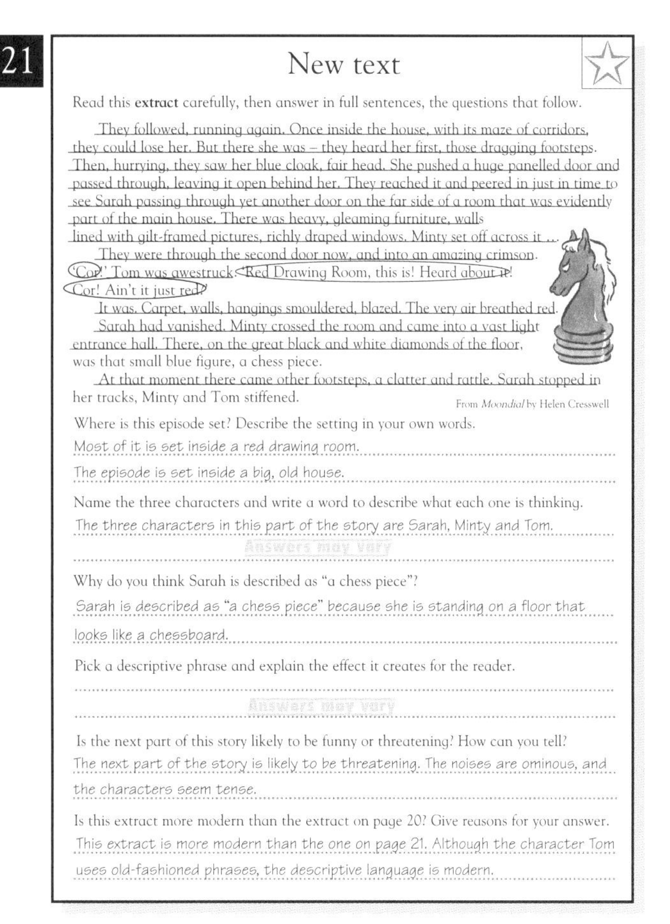

21

New text

Read this **extract** carefully, then answer in full sentences, the questions that follow.

They followed, running again. Once inside the house, with its maze of corridors, they could lose her. But there she was – they heard her first, those dragging footsteps. Then, hurrying, they saw her blue cloak, fair head. She pushed a huge panelled door and passed through, leaving it open behind her. They reached it and peered in just in time to see Sarah passing through yet another door on the far side of a room that was evidently part of the main house. There was heavy, gleaming furniture, walls lined with gilt-framed pictures, richly draped windows. Minty set off across it …

They were through the second door now, and into an amazing crimson.

'Cor!' Tom was awestruck. 'Red Drawing Room, this is! Heard about it! Cor! Ain't it just red?'

It was. Carpet, walls, hangings smouldered, blazed. The very air breathed red.

Sarah had vanished. Minty crossed the room and came into a vast light entrance hall. There, on the great black and white diamonds of the floor, was that small blue figure, a chess piece.

At that moment there came other footsteps, a clatter and rattle. Sarah stopped in her tracks, Minty and Tom stiffened.

From *Moondial* by Helen Cresswell

Where is this episode set? Describe the setting in your own words.

Most of it is set inside a red drawing room.

The episode is set inside a big, old house.

Name the three characters and write a word to describe what each one is thinking.

The three characters in this part of the story are Sarah, Minty and Tom.

Answers may vary

Why do you think Sarah is described as "a chess piece"?

Sarah is described as "a chess piece" because she is standing on a floor that looks like a chessboard.

Pick a descriptive phrase and explain the effect it creates for the reader.

Answers may vary

Is the next part of this story likely to be funny or threatening? How can you tell?

The next part of the story is likely to be threatening. The noises are ominous, and the characters seem tense.

Is this extract more modern than the extract on page 20? Give reasons for your answer.

This extract is more modern than the one on page 21. Although the character Tom uses old-fashioned phrases, the descriptive language is modern.

This page features a modern extract that shares a similar theme to the older extract on page 20. Talk about the text together before your child answers the questions. Check your child's handwriting, and point out areas that need further practice.

22

Comparing texts

Use the following questions to help you **plan** a **comparison** of the **extracts** on pages 20 and 21.

Underline the words of the **narrator** in both extracts. Write a sentence comparing them.

Answers may vary

Draw a ring around the **conversations** in both extracts. What differences can you see?

Answers may vary

Compare the **styles** of the two authors (their particular way of writing).

Answers may vary

Which of these terms could be used for the stories: **traditional**, **fantasy**, **novel**, **adventure**, **autobiography**, **romance**, **historical**? Explain your answer.

Answers may vary

Would you like to read more of either of these books? Which one and why?

Answers may vary

Describe a dramatic experience in the style of either writer.
Remember to use **paragraphs**.
Begin here, and continue on a separate sheet of paper.

Answers may vary

This page enables your child to write in detail about his or her response to the texts on pages 20 and 21. It may be helpful to talk about the questions with your child: this will help provoke the sort of discussion that takes place in a classroom.

23

Reported speech

Rewrite the following text in **reported speech**. It has been started for you. Continue on a separate sheet of paper if necessary.
Remember: **Reported speech** reports what the characters have said, rather than quoting their actual words. **Reported speech** is in the **past tense** and has no speech marks.

The Queen propped her up against a tree, and said kindly, "You may rest a little, now."

Alice looked round her in great surprise. "Why, I do believe weve been under this tree the whole time! Everything's just as it was!"

"Of course it is," said the Queen: "what would you have it"?

"Well, in *our* country," said Alice, still panting a little, "you'd generally get to somewhere else – if you ran very fast for a long time, as we've been doing."

"A slow sort of country!" said the Queen. "Now, *here*, you see, it takes all the running *you* can do, to keep in the same place. If you want to get somewhere else, you must run at least twice as fast as that!"

"I'd rather not try, please!" said Alice. "I'm quite content to stay here – only I *am* so hot and thirsty!"

"I know what *you'd* like!" the Queen said good-naturedly, taking a little box out of her pocket. "Have a biscuit?"

From *Through the Looking Glass* by Lewis Carroll

The Queen propped her up against a tree and told her kindly that she could rest a little. Alice looked around her and said with surprise, that she believed they had been under that tree all the time and everything had stayed just as it was. The Queen replied that of course it had and asked Alice what else she would want it to be. Alice explained, still panting slightly, that in her country people generally reached somewhere else if they ran fast for a long time as they had. The Queen declared that Alice's must be a slow sort of country. In hers, you had to run as fast as you could just to stay in one place and you needed to run twice as fast to get anywhere else. Alice said that she would rather not try and she was happy to stay where she was except that she was hot and thirsty. The Queen said she knew what Alice would like and asked her if she wanted a biscuit.

Most authors use a mixture of **reported** and **direct speech**. Why do you think they do this?

Using reported speech can help the story to flow and save space. Direct speech gives a sense of "being there".

This page provides your child with practice in converting direct speech into reported speech and examines the stylistic reasons for choosing one form or the other. Check that your child's rewriting of the passage is grammatically correct.

24

Character development

Reread the extracts on pages 20 and 23.

What are the good qualities about the Red Queen?

Answers may vary

What are the bad qualities about the Red Queen?

Answers may vary

Read this extract from a later chapter.

Everything was happening so oddly that she didn't feel a bit surprised at finding the Red Queen and the White Queen sitting close to her, one on each side: she would have liked very much to ask them how they came there, but she feared it would not be quite civil. However, there would be no harm, she thought, in asking if the game was over. "Please, would you tell me – " she began, looking timidly at the Red Queen.

"Speak when you're spoken to!" the Queen sharply interrupted her.

"But if everybody obeyed that rule," said Alice, who was always ready for a little argument, "and if you only spoke when you were spoken to, and the other person always waited for *you* to begin, you see nobody would ever say anything, so that – " "Ridiculous!" cried the Queen. "Why, don't you see, child –" here she broke off with a frown, and, after thinking for a minute, suddenly changed the subject of the conversation. "What do you mean by 'If you really are a Queen'? What right have you to all yourself so? You can't be a Queen, you know, till you've passed the proper examination. And the sooner we begin it, the better."

From *Through the Looking Glass* by Lewis Carroll

What qualities does the Red Queen have in this extract?

Answers may vary

If you met the Red Queen what would you like to ask her?

Answers may vary

At the end of the book, the Red Queen changes into Alice's pet kitten.
Why may the Red Queen be like a kitten?

Answers may vary

This activity challenges your child to consider a character's qualities and how an author has conveyed this. Imagining meeting a character helps to engage further. For the last question, your child should think about the qualities of a kitten, too.

25

Introducing characters

Pirates feature in many popular stories. Pirate characters have also appeared on stage, in film and on television. Now it is your turn to create a script with pirates as the main characters.
This planning sheet will help you to get started. Make brief notes only.

Setting – time and place (Will the scene take place in the past, present or future? Is it set on Earth or elsewhere?)

Answers may vary

Characters – about three or four only (Who are your characters? What are their good and bad qualities? How will you interest your audience in them?)

Answers may vary

Plot – what happens (What events or actions take place? How do the characters react to these events?)

Answers may vary

Write your script on a separate sheet of paper. Before you write, you will need to have a clear idea of what happens at the beginning and end of your scene. Also remember to give directions for the camera and for the characters actions. Write the dialogue next to the characters names (without speech marks).

On this page your child learns to write a play script. Check that your child understands that a play script has no narrator and the emphasis should be on dialogue. The qualities of each character need to be shown through the dialogue.

26

A questionnaire

Complete this brief **questionnaire** about your reading.

Fiction

Tick the types of **fiction** that you enjoy reading.

novels ☐ short stories ☐ science fiction ☐ historical ☐
adventure ☐ mystery ☐ fantasy ☐ others ....

My favourite **authors** are ....

My favourite **fiction** titles are ....

Answers may vary

Poetry

Tick the types of **poems** that you enjoy.

ballads ☐ haiku ☐ cinquain ☐ free verse ☐
limericks ☐ shape poems ☐ others ....

My favourite **poets** are ....

My favourite **poems** are ....

Answers may vary

Non-fiction

Tick the types of **non-fiction** that you enjoy reading.

sports ☐ games ☐ hobbies ☐ animal care ☐ computers ☐
science ☐ art ☐ music ☐ TV, film, etc. ☐ others ....

My favourite **non-fiction** titles are ....

Answers may vary

Now write more about your favourite types of reading on a separate sheet of paper. Try to persuade other people of your age to read the books or poems that you enjoy the most. Take care with your **punctuation**, **spelling** and **handwriting**.

On this page your child is asked to analyse his or her reading preferences and to write persuasively for a particular readership. Encourage your child to write in paragraphs and to check his or her finished writing for spelling and punctuation errors.

27

Prefixes

Read the following list of **prefixes**, then write the **prefixes** in **alphabetical order**.
Remember: A **prefix** is a group of letters added to the beginning of a word to change its meaning.

post- ante- kilo- pro- geo- bio- retro- vari- zoo- multi-
hydro- sub- extra- ultra- fore- peri- iso- contra- thermo-

ante-, bio-, contra-, extra-, fore-, geo-, hydro-, iso-, kilo-, multi-,
peri-, post-, pro-, retro-, sub-, thermo-, ultra-, vari-, zoo-

Use a **dictionary** to find a word beginning with each of the **prefixes** listed above. Write each word in a sentence that shows its meaning.

antechamber: We came to a small antechamber before entering the main hall.

Answers may vary

The activities on this page focus on the use of prefixes and help to extend vocabulary through word-building. There is also a chance to practise alphabetical ordering. Check that your child's sentences use the completed words correctly.

28

Suffixes

Follow the instructions below for each of the words in this list.

artist, importance, stationary, changeable, lioness
sorrowful, telegraph, clarify, advertise, magnetism
senseless, skilfully, happiness, headship, attitude
motion, cruelty, otherwise, pomposity

1 Write the word in the first column of the **chart**.
2 Decide which part of the word is its **suffix**, and write it in the second column.
3 Think of another word with the same **suffix**, and check its spelling in a dictionary.
4 Write the new word in the third column of the **chart**.
Remember: A **suffix** is a group of letters added to the end of a word to change its meaning.

Word	Suffix	New word
artist	-ist	chemist
importance	-ance	
stationary	-ary	
changeable	-able	
lioness	-ess	
sorrowful	-ful	
telegraph	-graph	
clarify	-ify	
advertise	-ise	
magnetism	-ism	
senseless	-less	
skilfully	-ly	
happiness	-ness	
headship	-ship	
attitude	-ude	
motion	-ion	
cruelty	-ty	
otherwise	-wise	
pomposity	-ity	

Answers may vary

This page extends your child's word-building skills with practice in the use of suffixes. In the last column of the chart, accept any word with the correct suffix.

29

Joining sentences

The **sentences** below are about the game of chess, but they are in the wrong order. Read through the **sentences** and decide on the best order.

Computers play chess. Chess remains popular today. There are sixteen pieces on each side. Chess is a game for two people. "Checkmate" means that the king cannot move without being taken by another piece. The board and the pieces can be in any two contrasting colours. Pieces move in different ways. Computers sometimes beat human champions. Chess is played on a chequered board. It seems complicated at first. Each side has one king, one queen, two knights, two bishops, two rooks and eight pawns. The board is usually black and white. The game ends when one of the kings is "checkmated". Experts improve their game by learning special patterns of moves. Chess is a very old game.

Write the sentences in order here.

1. Chess is a very old game.
2. Chess remains popular today.
3. Computers play chess.
4. Computers sometimes beat human champions.
5. Chess is a game for two people.
6. Chess is played on a chequered board.
7. The board is usually black and white.
8. The board and the pieces can be any two contrasting colours.
9. There are sixteen pieces on each side.
10. Each side has one king, one queen, two knights, two bishops, two rooks and eight pawns.
11. Pieces move in different ways.
12. It seems complicated at first.
13. Experts improve their game by learning special patterns of moves.
14. "Checkmate" means that the king cannot move without being taken by another piece.
15. The game ends when one of the kings is "checkmated".

All these **sentences** about chess are very short. **Join** some of the **sentences** to make the piece of writing read more fluently. You may need to add, remove or change some words, but make sure you keep all the main ideas. Write out your **sentences** on a separate sheet of paper.

Here your child practises organising information. Remind your child about some connecting words and phrases that he or she could use. Your child's finished writing should read fluently and contain all the main points from the original.

30

Active and passive

Active sentences describe an action done **by the subject.**
I directed the award-winning film. (an **active** sentence)
Passive sentences describe an action done **to the subject.**
The award-winning film was directed by me. (a **passive** sentence)

Change these sentences from **passive** to **active**.

The match was won by our team.
Our team won the match.

The winning goal was scored by Rachel.
Rachel scored the winning goal.

The party was enjoyed by all my friends.
All my friends enjoyed the party.

Jack was stung by an unusual insect.
An unusual insect stung Jack.

Now change these sentences from **active** to **passive**.

Aliens invade our planet.
Our planet is invaded by aliens.

Leonardo da Vinci painted the *Mona Lisa*.
The Mona Lisa was painted by Leonardo da Vinci.

The team dislike the group leader.
The group leader is disliked by the team.

The hero piloted his craft with great skill.
The hero's craft was piloted with great skill.

A hurricane struck the town.
The town was struck by a hurricane.

Here the task is to change a sentence from active to passive and *vice versa*. Check that your child understands the difference between the active and passive voices and can use them confidently. It may help if you think up practice sentences together.

31

Colons, semicolons and dashes

Punctuation can be used to connect groups of words. The **punctuation marks** that do this are: the **colon (:)**, the **semicolon (;)** and the **dash (–)**.

Read each sentence below, and write another sentence using the same **punctuation marks**.
Remember:

- A **colon** is used to introduce a list, a quotation or a second clause that makes the first clause easier to understand. (A clause is a group of words with a verb in it.)
- A **semicolon** is used to link complete clauses that are too closely related to separate with a full stop.
  It can also be used to separate items in a list that already has commas in it.
- A **dash** can be used to separate a comment from the rest of a sentence. It makes a stronger break than a comma and is less formal than brackets.

Bring these things with you: a jumper, your swimsuit, your lunch and your bus fare.

It was Shakespeare's Juliet who asked: "What's in a name?"

The match was abandoned: rain poured down.

We had to stop playing: I went to Matt's house.

I bought a kilo of big, juicy apples; two large, ripe lemons; a grapefruit and a punnet of delicious, sweet-smelling strawberries.

The weather is lovely – wish you were here!

These sentences help your child explore the use of colons, semicolons and dashes. Children often find these sophisticated punctuation marks very difficult to use, so you may need to offer help. Accept any sentences with the correct punctuation.

32

Word search

Find the 12 words below in the word search.

p	a	v	e	r	a	g	e	l	c
r	v	c	a	q	u	e	u	e	o
o	a	e	c	p	s	r	o	i	m
g	r	s	h	o	y	a	m	s	m
r	i	o	i	e	m	s	m	u	u
a	e	c	e	h	b	p	e	r	n
m	t	c	v	p	o	v	a	e	i
m	y	u	e	y	l	o	s	n	t
e	s	p	e	c	i	a	l	l	y
s	s	y	s	t	e	m	e	y	n

Learn these words.

programme especially community accompany symbol achieve

average variety occupy leisure queue system

Choose six words. Write a sentence for each one to show its meaning.

Word searches are a fun way for your child to revise spelling and to learn tricky spelling patterns. Encourage your child to write each word in a sentence that conveys how it is used rather than just a definition.